T0312372

A PARTRIDGE IN A PEAR TREE

A PARTRIDGE IN A PEAR TREE

Crochet the 12 Birds of Christmas

@TOFT_UK

PAVILION

CONTENTS

INTRODUCTION

The Twelve Days of Christmas is a song that many of us will have learned at school, and my children love nothing more than belting out 'five gold rings' for the whole of December.

There is much research and discussion over the symbolism and meaning of the song, and I have chosen to interpret the twelve gifts of true-love as birds. From the obvious Partridge in a Pear Tree through to the drumming of the Woodpecker, you can crochet your own way through the verses and create your own collection of birds. Enjoy making them to give as gifts, for a stunning festive mantelpiece decoration or even to hang on wreaths, trees and shelves around your home.

Edward's Menagerie has been a large part of my life for the last eight years, with daily inspiration provided by the stories of people learning to crochet – it feels like my crochet animal patterns are spreading some happiness all over the world. I am as hooked as everyone else on crocheting the next animal pattern in the collection – and Christmas is one of the best times of year to share some joy with what you can make with, and for, others.

The patterns in this book are designed for you and your friends and family to enjoy and are for private use only. I can't wait to see photos once you start making these so please don't forget to share them and use the #edsanimals tag so that I can enjoy seeing them, and you can share in everyone else's crochet adventures too.

Wishing you and your families a very Merry Christmas, and may you have lots of fun making and playing with these birds. **Enjoy.**

MY PROJECT BAG

All the birds in this book are made using TOFT pure wool in a double knitting weight and a 3mm hook. Each bird weighs around 60–80g, and the colours are written on the project pages in order of the quantity used within that pattern.

To make all of the birds in this book in TOFT double knitting you would need:

Cream 200g	Ruby 50g
Charcoal 200g	Orange 50g
Oatmeal 150g	Yellow 50g
Chestnut 100g	Silver 50g
Camel 100g	Fudge 25g
Shale 75g	Steel 25g
Stone 75g	Green 25g
Black 50g	

MATERIALS

YOU WILL NEED

YARN in appropriate colours and quantities (see individual patterns)

CROCHET HOOK in an appropriate size to match the yarn and your tension

STUFFING material

SEWING needle

EYES use black yarn as shown or safety eye alternative

SCISSORS

TOFT YARNS

I have had the pleasure of selecting, designing and manufacturing luxury yarns for the past twelve years, and these birds have been crocheted entirely in TOFT yarn. TOFT yarns are luxury, quality, natural fibres manufactured to my distinctive specifications here in the UK. When crocheted in TOFT yarns the projects are supple and soft but with a closed fabric to hide the stuffing inside.

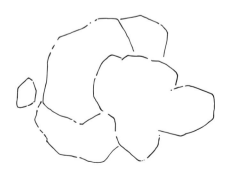
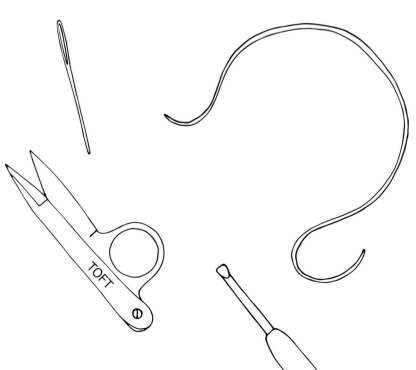

HOW TO USE

SKILL LEVELS

The patterns in this book are arranged in order of the song, but each has a SKILL LEVEL to indicate the complexity of the techniques involved.

- **Level one** (beginner) birds are the easiest with the biggest challenge being the splitting technique used for the feet, but everything else should be straightforward once you've learned your double crochet stitch.

- **Level two** (easy) patterns will have more colour changing involved in the pattern, but will move cleanly from one yarn to the next at the end of a rnd.

- **Level three** (intermediate) patterns will require more concentration and include disciplined colour changing moving backwards and forwards between the yarns. Mastering loop stitch will also be required for some of the more advanced projects.

The levels are intended to be encouraging, not off-putting, and serve to ensure that as a newbie to this fun craft, you pick something that will be a bit easier going as you master counting your stitches, holding your yarn and remembering to keep track of where you are in the pattern at the same time. I must emphasise that all of the techniques used are easy – the only thing that makes some of them very demanding is the discipline involved in accurately counting your way through the pattern. I know when learning to do a new thing it is nice to be reassured you are not accidentally trying to run before you can walk (but by all means if you are one of those people who are happy to push themselves then flick the pages and dive in!).

INTERNATIONAL TERMS

The patterns all use British English crochet terms, primarily the double crochet (US single crochet) stitch. Please refer to the CROCHET BASICS section (see page 12) for US explanations.

SAFETY

Your bird will only be as child-safe as you make it, so don't skimp on the stitches when sewing up. I sew all the way around the edges of any part I am sewing into position. If opting to use safety eyes, buttons or beads please be aware that these should not be used on a toy for a child under five years of age. For these young children you should always embroider the eyes on.

CROCHET BASICS

For further help learning to crochet, see videos at www.toftuk.com.

TENSION

Edward's Menagerie was inspired by TOFT yarn, and all of the animals in this book have been created in TOFT's pure wool double knitting (DK) yarn and a 3mm hook, but all the patterns will also work with thinner and thicker yarns. The required quantity of yarn needed in the projects is based on using TOFT DK yarns. If using other brands of yarn, the quantities may vary significantly depending on the fibre composition and spinning specifications of the yarn. If you are seeing holes in your fabric when working the patterns, swap your hook size down half a millimetre. Likewise, if your work is too solid and you are finding the stitches hard to work then swap up by half a millimetre. The standard tension of TOFT DK yarn on a 3mm hook is 3 x 3cm = 6 sts x 7 rnds.

MARKING

I always view stitch marking as a bit of a lifeline when I crochet. I recommend using a piece of contrast yarn, approximately 15cm long, positioned after the end of Round 2; once you have 12 sts it is easier to see where to place it. As you return back round to your marker, pull it forwards or backwards through or between your stitches to weave the marker up the fabric. Should you ever complete a round and discover you don't have the correct number of stitches (or even have to abandon what you are making mid-round and forget where you are), you can always return to your last stitch marking.

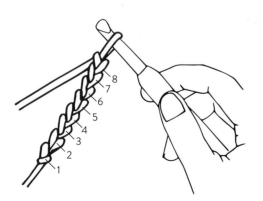

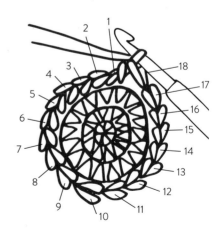

TECHNIQUES

RIGHT-HANDED HOLD

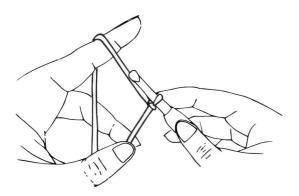

LEFT-HANDED HOLD

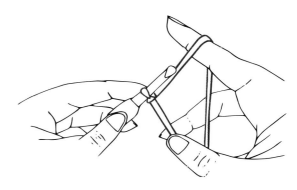

SLIP KNOT

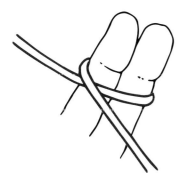

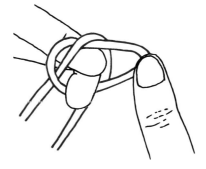

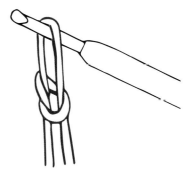

1 Wrap the yarn around your fingers

2 Pull the tail end of the yarn through the wrap to make a loop.

3 Place your hook through the loop and tighten, ensuring that it is the tail end of the yarn (not the ball end) that controls the opening and closing of the knot.

CHAIN STITCH (CH)

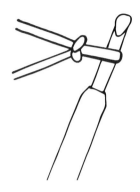

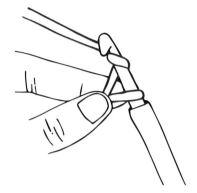

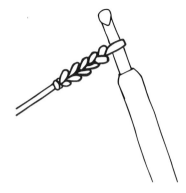

1 Make a slip knot.

2 Wrap the yarn over the hook (yarn over) and pull it through the loop on the hook.

3 Repeat until desired length.

DC6 INTO RING (MAGIC CIRCLE)

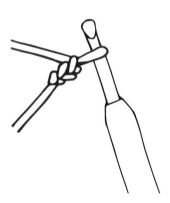

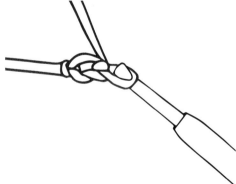

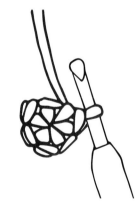

1 Make a slip knot and chain two stitches.

2 Insert the hook into the first chain stitch made and work a double crochet six times into it.

3 Pull tightly on the tail of the yarn to close the centre of the ring and form a neat circle.

DOUBLE CROCHET STITCH (DC)

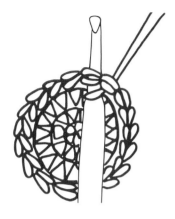 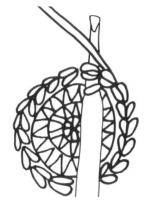 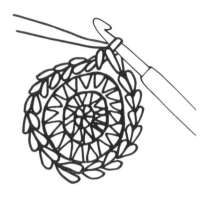

1 Insert the hook through the stitch under both loops of the 'V' unless otherwise stated.

2 Yarn over, rotate hook head, and pull through the stitch (two loops on hook).

3 Yarn over again and pull through both loops on the hook to end with one loop on the hook (one double crochet stitch made).

DECREASING (DC2TOG)

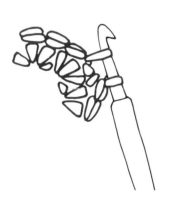 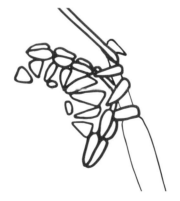 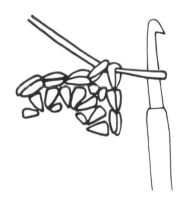

1 Insert the hook under the front loop only of the next stitch (two loops on hook).

2 In the same motion insert the hook through the front loop only of the following stitch.

3 Yarn over and pull through the first two loops on the hook, then yarn over and pull through both loops.

COLOUR CHANGE

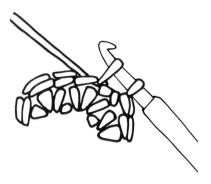 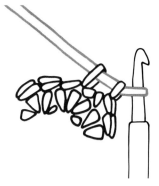 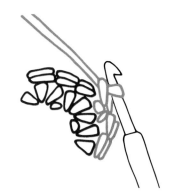

1 Insert the hook through the next stitch, yarn over and pull through the stitch (two loops on hook).

2 Yarn over with the new colour and complete the double crochet stitch with this new yarn.

3 Continue with this new yarn, leaving the original yarn at the back of the work. Cut the original yarn if this is a one-off colour change, or run it along the back of the fabric if returning to it later.

SPLITTING THE ROUND

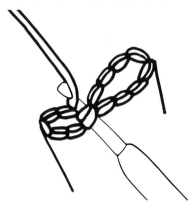 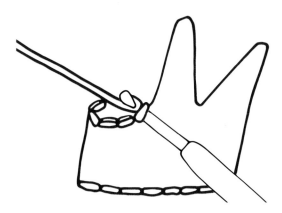

1 Count back the required number of stitches from your hook to split the round as instructed in the pattern. Cross the round and double crochet into this stitch from the right side of the fabric to create two smaller rounds.

2 Work the stitches on the first smaller round as instructed. Once completed, rejoin the yarn and work the other smaller rounds.

CHAIN AND THEN SLIP STITCH TO JOIN INTO CIRCLE

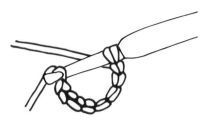  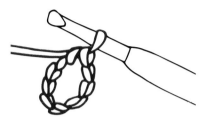

1 Chain the stated number of stitches, then insert the hook into the back of the stitch closest to the slipknot, ensuring not to twist the stitches.

2 Yarn over the hook.

3 Pull the yarn through the stitch and the loop on the hook in one motion.

LOOP STITCH

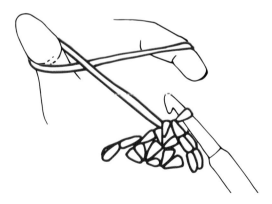 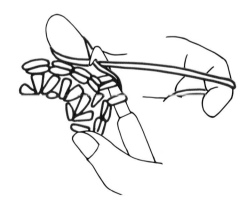

1 Insert the hook through the stitch. Wrap the yarn from front to back over the thumb of your non-hook hand and yarn over with the yarn behind your thumb.

2 Hold the loop on your thumb and complete the double crochet stitch.

SLIP STITCH TRAVERSE

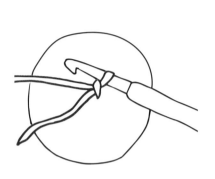
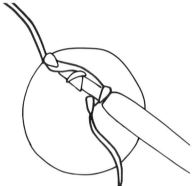
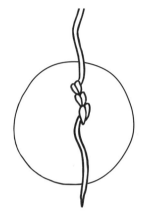

1 Insert the hook into the fabric around a stitch or row.

2 Yarn over and pull through the stitch and all loops on the hook (one slip stitch made).

3 Repeat in desired direction, moving across the surface of the fabric.

CHAIN LOOPS

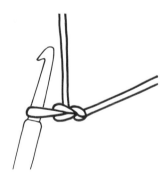
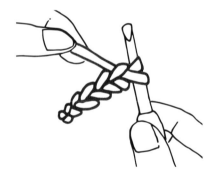
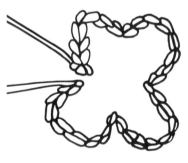

1 Insert the hook through the fabric at the desired position, yarn over and pull through the fabric.

2 Chain the number of stitches stated in the pattern.

3 Attach the chain to the fabric with a slip stitch approximately two stitches or two rounds away from the start of the chain. Repeat until the required area is covered.

SLIP STITCH CHAINS

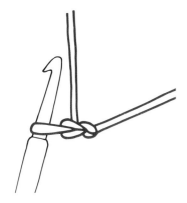

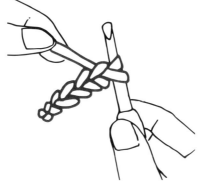

1 Insert the hook through the fabric at the desired position, yarn over and pull through the fabric.

2 Chain the number of stitches stated in the pattern.

3 Working back down the chain, insert the hook into the next stitch.

SLIP STITCH TRAVERSE ROOT

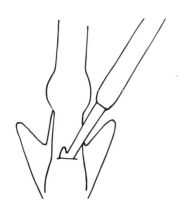

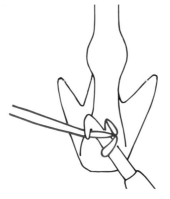

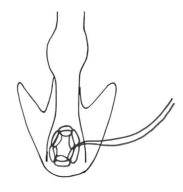

1 Insert hook into the fabric around a st.

2 Yarn over and pull through the loop in one motion (slip stitch).

3 Move across the fabric in a circle making X sts in a round to create a root to then double crochet into.

FINISHING

SEWING UP

To keep each pattern concise I have omitted all the general stuffing and sewing-up instructions from the pattern if they are common to all. I am not a believer in stuffing the parts as I go along as I find I sometimes then end up working bits of stuffing into my stitches and the weight of the piece impacts my tension.

When stuffing your birds less is definitely more. You want to show off the shape of the body and not make them firm and stiff, and so proceed with caution and stuff tiny pinches of fluff into the thighs.

STUFFING THE BODIES

All the bodies are stuffed gently to fill out the shape, neck and chest, but retain their supple feel.

STUFFING THE HEADS

All the heads are stuffed at the point at which you decrease to 9 sts. Any stuffing required on beaks, crowns and combs will be detailed in the individual patterns.

STUFFING THE LEGS AND FINISHING THE FEET

While it is not essential to stuff the thighs of any of the birds, on some it will be recommended in the pattern that you do so.

TAILS

Finish the tail by sewing your chain stitch start flat and closed and then oversew the tail onto the back horizontally.

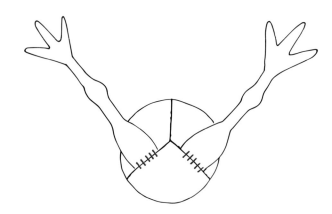

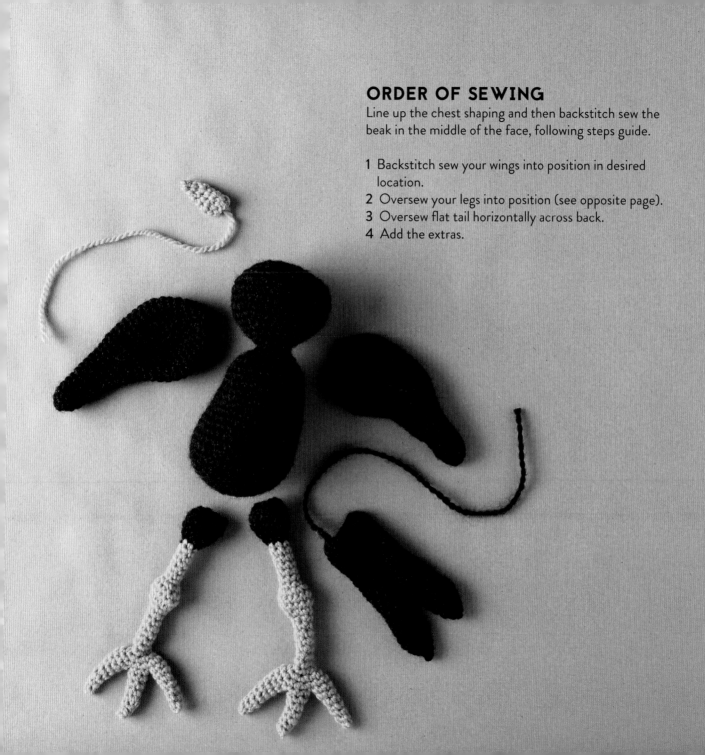

ORDER OF SEWING

Line up the chest shaping and then backstitch sew the beak in the middle of the face, following steps guide.

1 Backstitch sew your wings into position in desired location.
2 Oversew your legs into position (see opposite page).
3 Oversew flat tail horizontally across back.
4 Add the extras.

1

FELIX
THE RED-LEGGED PARTRIDGE

Having spent twelve months diligently practising his
'ho, ho, ho' every morning in the shower, Felix feels like
he's fully rehearsed and ready to become one of Santa's little
helpers this year. Although he attempted it, growing a beard
beyond a light smattering of stubble proved too much of a
challenge, so instead he's heavily invested in a magnificent real
yak hair beard, which he's conscientiously oiled to a stunning
sheen these last few weeks. Regardless of his suspicions about
whether that may have made it to the Naughty or Nice list, he's
got smiles for everyone as he asks all the children what they
would like to find under the tree this Christmas.

BODY/NECK/HEAD
Working in Camel
Begin by dc6 into ring
Rnd 1 (dc2 into next st) 6 times (12 sts)
Rnd 2 (dc1, dc2 into next st) 6 times (18)
Rnd 3 (dc2, dc2 into next st) 6 times (24)
Rnd 4 (dc3, dc2 into next st) 6 times (30)
Rnd 5 (dc4, dc2 into next st) 6 times (36)
Rnd 6 (dc5, dc2 into next st) 6 times (42)
Rnd 7 dc
Change to Shale
Rnds 8-9 dc (2 rnds)
Rnd 10 (dc5, dc2tog) 6 times (36)
Rnds 11-14 dc (4 rnds)
Rnd 15 (dc4, dc2tog) 6 times (30)
Rnds 16-17 dc (2 rnds)
Change to Cream
Rnd 18 dc
Rnd 19 (dc4 Cream, dc1 Charcoal) 6 times
Rnd 20 (dc3, dc2tog) 6 times Cream (24)
Rnd 21 dc Cream
Rnd 22 dc3 Cream, dc2tog Charcoal, (dc2tog) 3 times Cream, dc2tog Charcoal, (dc2tog) 3 times Cream, dc2tog Charcoal, dc3 Cream (15)
Rnd 23 (dc2tog) 5 times, dc5 Cream (10)
Change to Charcoal
Rnd 24 dc
Rnd 25 (dc2 into next st) 10 times (20)
Rnd 26 (dc3, dc2 into next st) 5 times (25)
Rnd 27 (dc4, dc2 into next st) 5 times (30)
Rnd 28 (dc2, dc2 into next st) 10 times (40)

Rnd 29 dc11 Charcoal, dc18 Cream, dc2 Charcoal, dc9 Shale
Rnds 30-32 dc9 Shale, dc2 Charcoal, dc18 Cream, dc2 Charcoal, dc9 Shale (3 rnds)
Rnd 33 dc7, dc2tog Shale, dc2 Charcoal, dc7, dc2tog, dc6, dc2tog Cream, dc2 Charcoal, dc8, dc2tog Shale (36)
Rnd 34 dc4, dc2tog, dc3 Shale, dc2 Charcoal, dc2tog, dc3, dc2tog, dc4, dc2tog, dc2 Cream, dc2 Charcoal, dc2tog, dc4, dc2tog Shale (30)
Rnd 35 dc3, dc2tog, dc3 Shale, dc2 Charcoal, (dc2tog, dc2) 3 times Cream, dc2 Charcoal, dc2tog, dc2, dc2tog Shale (24)
Change to Camel
Rnd 36 (dc2, dc2tog) 6 times (18)
Rnd 37 dc
Rnd 38 (dc2tog) 9 times (9)
Rnd 39 (dc1, dc2tog) 3 times (6)

LEGS (make two)
Working in Camel
Ch12 and sl st to join into a circle
Rnds 1-3 dc (3 rnds)
Rnd 4 (dc2, dc2tog) 3 times (9)
Rnd 5 (dc1, dc2tog) 3 times (6)
Change to Ruby
Rnds 6-8 dc (3 rnds)
Rnd 9 (dc2 into next st) 6 times (12)
Rnds 10-11 dc (2 rnds)
Rnd 12 (dc2tog) 6 times (6)
Rnds 13-16 dc (4 rnds)

Rnd 17 (dc2 into next st) 6 times (12)

Rnd 18 (dc1, dc2 into next st) 6 times (18)

Split into three rnds of 6 sts and work each as follows:

Rnds 1-3 dc (3 rnds)

Rnd 4 dc2tog, dc4 (5)

Rnd 5 dc

Rnd 6 dc2tog, dc3 (4)

BACK DIGIT (optional)

SLIP STITCH TRAVERSE (see page 19) a 6-st root on
   back of foot and work as follows:

Rnd 1 dc

Rnd 2 dc2tog, dc4 (5)

Rnd 3 dc

Rnd 4 dc2tog, dc3 (4)

Lightly stuff thigh and sew flat across top to close.

WINGS (make two)

Starting in Cream work 1 rnd Cream, 1 rnd Chestnut (dc6
   into ring always counts as first rnd)

Begin by dc6 into ring

Rnd 1 (dc2 into next st) 6 times (12)

Rnd 2 (dc1, dc2 into next st) 6 times (18)

Rnd 3 (dc2, dc2 into next st) 6 times (24)

Rnds 4-5 dc (2 rnds)

Rnd 6 (dc2, dc2tog) 6 times (18)

Rnds 7-8 dc (2 rnds)

Rnd 9 (dc4, dc2tog) 3 times (15)

Rnd 10 dc

Rnd 11 (dc1, dc2tog) 5 times (10)

Rnds 12-13 dc (2 rnds)

Rnd 14 (dc2tog) 5 times (5)

Do not stuff.

BEAK

Working in Ruby

Ch12 and sl st to join into a circle

Rnds 1-2 dc (2 rnds)

Rnd 3 (dc2, dc2tog) 3 times (9)

Rnd 4 (dc1, dc2tog) 3 times (6)

Rnd 5 dc

Rnd 6 (dc2tog) 3 times (3)

Stuff lightly and sew into position.

EYE PATCHES (make two)

Working in Ruby

Begin by dc6 into ring

Rnd 1 (dc1, dc2 into next st) 3 times (9)

Sew into position.

TAIL

Working in Shale

Ch16 and sl st to join into a circle

Rnd 1 dc

Rnds 2-6 dc (5 rnds)

Split into two rnds of 8 sts and work each as follows:

Rnds 1-4 dc (4 rnds)

Rnd 5 dc7, dc2 into next (9)

Rnds 6-7 dc (2 rnds)

Rnd 8 (dc2, dc2 into next st) 3 times (12)

Rnds 9-10 dc (2 rnds)

Rnd 11 (dc2, dc2tog) 3 times (9)

Rnd 12 (dc1, dc2tog) 3 times (6)

Do not stuff.

Finish by sewing eyes into place with Black yarn.

2

BEATRICE
THE TURTLE DOVE

Beatrice has twenty-four grandchildren (and that number is not showing any signs of plateauing). Every year since the birth of her first granddaughter she has upheld her own Christmas tradition of knitting each child a new stocking to hang off the mantelpiece. With every new ultrasound scan she's sent to adorn her fridge, her Christmas custom becomes an increased challenge. No longer requiring any kind of pattern, she can turn a heel on anything in a jiffy, mastering cables, Fair Isle and every other technique she can get her hands on to go onto her latest giant sock. If this Christmas brings an announcement of the pitter-patter of tiny feet once again, she might treat herself just to the one week off, before casting on the first one on New Year's Day.

BODY/NECK/HEAD

Working in Oatmeal

Begin by dc6 into ring

Rnd 1 (dc2 into next st) 6 times (12 sts)

Rnd 2 (dc1, dc2 into next st) 6 times (18)

Rnd 3 (dc2, dc2 into next st) 6 times (24)

Rnd 4 (dc3, dc2 into next st) 6 times (30)

Rnd 5 (dc4, dc2 into next st) 6 times (36)

Rnd 6 (dc5, dc2 into next st) 6 times (42)

Rnds 7-9 dc (3 rnds)

Rnd 10 (dc5, dc2tog) 6 times (36)

Rnds 11-14 dc (4 rnds)

Rnd 15 (dc4, dc2tog) 6 times (30)

Rnds 16-19 dc (4 rnds)

Rnd 20 (dc3, dc2tog) 6 times (24)

Rnd 21 dc

Stuff and continue

Rnd 22 (dc2tog) 9 times Oatmeal, dc6 Cream (15)

Rnd 23 (dc2tog) 4 times Oatmeal, dc2tog, dc5 Charcoal (10)

Rnd 24 dc1 Charcoal, dc4 Oatmeal, dc5 Cream

Rnd 25 dc1 into next st Cream, dc1 into same st Oatmeal, (dc2 into next st) 4 times Oatmeal, (dc2 into next st) 5 times Charcoal (20)

Rnd 26 dc2 Charcoal, dc1, dc2 into next st, dc3, dc2 into next st, dc2 Oatmeal, dc1, dc2 into next st, (dc3, dc2 into next st) twice Cream (25)

Rnd 27 dc3 Cream, dc1, dc2 into next st, dc4, dc2 into next st, dc2 Oatmeal, dc2, dc2 into next st, (dc4, dc2 into next st) twice Charcoal (30)

Rnd 28 dc2, dc2 into next st Charcoal, (dc2, dc2 into next st) 9 times Oatmeal (40)

Continue in Oatmeal

Rnds 29-31 dc (3 rnds)

Rnd 32 (dc8, dc2tog) 4 times (36)

Rnd 33 dc

Rnd 34 (dc4, dc2tog) 6 times (30)

Rnd 35 (dc3, dc2tog) 6 times (24)

Rnd 36 (dc2, dc2tog) 6 times (18)

Rnd 37 dc

Rnd 38 (dc2tog) 9 times (9)

Rnd 39 (dc1, dc2tog) 3 times (6)

LEGS (make two)

Working in Oatmeal

Ch12 and sl st to join into a circle

Rnds 1-3 dc (3 rnds)

Rnd 4 (dc2, dc2tog) 3 times (9)

Rnd 5 (dc1, dc2tog) 3 times (6)

Change to Stone

Rnds 6-11 dc (6 rnds)

Rnd 12 (dc2 into next st) 6 times (12)

Rnds 13-14 dc (2 rnds)

Rnd 15 (dc2tog) 6 times (6)

Rnds 16-22 dc (7 rnds)

Rnd 23 (dc2 into next st) 6 times (12)

Rnd 24 (dc1, dc2 into next st) 6 times (18)

Split into three rnds of 6 sts and work each as follows:

Rnds 1-3 dc (3 rnds)

Rnd 4 dc2tog, dc4 (5)

Rnds 5-6 dc (2 rnds)

Rnd 7 dc2tog, dc3 (4)

BACK DIGIT (optional)

SLIP STITCH TRAVERSE (see page 19) a 6-st root on
  back of foot and work as follows:

Rnd 1 dc

Rnd 2 dc2tog, dc4 (5)

Rnds 3-4 dc (2 rnds)

Rnd 5 dc2tog, dc3 (4)

Lightly stuff thigh and sew flat across top to close.

WINGS (make two)

Working in Charcoal

Begin by dc6 into ring

Rnd 1 (dc1, dc2 into next st) 3 times (9)

Rnd 2 dc8, dc2 into next st (10)

Rnd 3 dc

Rnd 4 dc9, dc2 into next st (11)

Rnd 5 dc

Rnd 6 dc10, dc2 into next st (12)

Change to working odd rnds in Camel and even rnds as 2
  sts Camel, 2 sts Charcoal

Rnd 7 dc

Rnd 8 dc11, dc2 into next st (13)

Rnd 9 dc

Rnd 10 dc12, dc2 into next st (14)

Rnd 11 dc

Rnd 12 (dc6, dc2 into next st) twice (16)

Rnd 13 dc2 into next st, dc14, dc2 into next st (18)

Rnd 14 dc2 into next st, dc16, dc2 into next st (20)

Rnd 15 dc2 into next st, dc18, dc2 into next st (22)

Rnd 16 dc2 into next st, dc20, dc2 into next st (24)

Rnd 17 dc2 into next st, dc22, dc2 into next st (26)

Rnds 18-21 dc (4 rnds)

Rnd 22 (dc11, dc2tog) twice (24)

Rnd 23 (dc2, dc2tog) 6 times (18)

Rnd 24 dc

Rnd 25 (dc1, dc2tog) 6 times (12)

Rnd 26 (dc2tog) 6 times (6)

Do not stuff.

BEAK

Working in Stone

Ch8 and sl st to join into a circle

Rnds 1-2 dc (2 rnds)

Rnd 3 (dc2, dc2tog) twice (6)

Rnds 4-5 dc (2 rnds)

Rnd 6 (dc2tog) 3 times (3)

Stuff lightly and sew into position.

TAIL

Working in Oatmeal

Ch16 and sl st to join into a circle

Rnds 1-5 dc (5 rnds)

Change to Charcoal

Rnd 6 dc

Change to Camel

Split into two rnds of 8 sts and work each as follows:

Rnds 1-3 dc (3 rnds)

Change to Charcoal

Rnd 4 dc

Change to Camel

Rnd 5 dc7, dc2 into next st (9)

Rnds 6-7 dc (2 rnds)

Continue in Charcoal

Rnd 8 dc8, dc2 into next st (10)

Rnds 9-10 dc (2 rnds)

Rnd 11 (dc4, dc2 into next st) twice (12)

Rnds 12-13 dc (2 rnds)

Rnd 14 (dc2tog) 6 times (6)

Do not stuff.

Finish by sewing eyes into place with Black yarn.

3

RUTH

THE FRENCH HEN

Ruth is adamant that this is the year she will finally perfect her eggnog technique and blow her neighbours away with the ultimate festive party tipple. She's whisking and folding her way to success, at the same time filling her house with all her favourite smells of cloves, nutmeg, cinnamon and vanilla. Embodying the warmth of a family Christmas around an open fire, Ruth likes hers with bourbon, but is ready and set to please everyone, having combined her frothy Christmas cloud with three different liquors. With that all sorted, there's just enough time for her pick out her most glitzy outfit, pour the snacks into bowls, and get ready to wish everyone a very Merry Christmas.

BODY/NECK/HEAD
Working in Oatmeal
Begin by dc6 into ring
Rnd 1 (dc2 into next st) 6 times (12 sts)
Rnd 2 (dc1, dc2 into next st) 6 times (18)
Rnd 3 (dc2, dc2 into next st) 6 times (24)
Rnd 4 (dc3, dc2 into next st) 6 times (30)
Rnd 5 (dc4, dc2 into next st) 6 times (36)
Rnd 6 (dc5, dc2 into next st) 6 times (42)
Rnds 7-9 dc (3 rnds)
Rnd 10 (dc5, dc2tog) 6 times (36)
Rnds 11-14 dc (4 rnds)
Rnd 15 (dc4, dc2tog) 6 times (30)
Rnds 16-19 dc (4 rnds)
Rnd 20 (dc3, dc2tog) 6 times (24)
Rnd 21 dc
Rnd 22 (dc2tog) 9 times, dc6 (15)
Rnd 23 (dc2tog) 5 times, dc5 (10)
Rnd 24 dc
Rnd 25 (dc2 into next st) 10 times (20)
Rnd 26 (dc3, dc2 into next st) 5 times (25)
Rnd 27 (dc4, dc2 into next st) 5 times (30)
Rnd 28 (dc2, dc2 into next st) 10 times (40)
Rnds 29-31 dc (3 rnds)
Rnd 32 (dc8, dc2tog) 4 times (36)
Rnd 33 dc
Rnd 34 (dc4, dc2tog) 6 times (30)
Rnd 35 (dc3, dc2tog) 6 times (24)
Rnd 36 (dc2, dc2tog) 6 times (18)
Rnd 37 dc
Rnd 38 (dc2tog) 9 times (9)
Rnd 39 (dc1, dc2tog) 3 times (6)

LEGS (make two)
Working in Oatmeal
Ch12 and sl st to join into a circle
Rnds 1-3 dc (3 rnds)
Rnd 4 (dc2, dc2tog) 3 times (9)
Rnd 5 (dc1, dc2tog) 3 times (6)
Change to Camel
Rnds 6-12 dc (7 rnds)
Rnd 13 (dc2 into next st) 6 times (12)
Rnds 14-15 dc (2 rnds)
Rnd 16 (dc2tog) 6 times (6)
Rnds 17-24 dc (8 rnds)
Rnd 25 (dc2 into next st) 6 times (12)
Rnd 26 (dc1, dc2 into next st) 6 times (18)
Split into three rnds of 6 sts and work each as follows:
Rnds 1-3 dc (3 rnds)
Rnd 4 dc2tog, dc4 (5)
Rnds 5-6 dc (2 rnds)
Rnd 7 dc2tog, dc3 (4)

BACK DIGIT (optional)
SLIP STITCH TRAVERSE (see page 19) a 6-st root on
    back of foot and work as follows:
Rnd 1 dc
Rnd 2 dc2tog, dc4 (5)
Rnds 3-4 dc (2 rnds)
Rnd 5 dc2tog, dc3 (4)
Lightly stuff thigh and sew flat across top to close.

WINGS (make two)

Working in Oatmeal

Begin by dc6 into ring

Rnd 1 (dc1, dc2 into next st) 3 times (9)

Rnd 2 dc8, dc2 into next st (10)

Rnd 3 dc

Rnd 4 dc9, dc2 into next st (11)

Rnd 5 dc

Rnd 6 dc10, dc2 into next st (12)

Rnd 7 dc

Rnd 8 dc11, dc2 into next st (13)

Rnd 9 dc

Rnd 10 dc12, dc2 into next st (14)

Rnd 11 dc

Rnd 12 (dc6, dc2 into next st) twice (16)

Rnd 13 dc2 into next st, dc14, dc2 into next st (18)

Rnd 14 dc2 into next st, dc16, dc2 into next st (20)

Rnd 15 dc2 into next st, dc18, dc2 into next st (22)

Rnd 16 dc2 into next st, dc20, dc2 into next st (24)

Rnd 17 dc2 into next st, dc22, dc2 into next st (26)

Rnds 18-21 dc (4 rnds)

Rnd 22 (dc11, dc2tog) twice (24)

Rnd 23 (dc2, dc2tog) 6 times (18)

Rnd 24 dc

Rnd 25 (dc1, dc2tog) 6 times (12)

Rnd 26 (dc2tog) 6 times (6)

Do not stuff.

BEAK

Working in Camel

Ch8 and sl st to join into circle

Rnds 1-2 dc (2 rnds)

Rnd 3 (dc2, dc2tog) twice (6)

Rnds 4-5 dc (2 rnds)

Rnd 6 (dc1, dc2tog) twice (4)

Stuff lightly and sew into position.

CREST

Working in Oatmeal

Work ch15 CHAIN LOOPS (see page 18) over top of the head.

TAIL

Working in Oatmeal

Work two rows of four ch24 CHAIN LOOPS in tail position.

Finish by sewing eyes into place with Black yarn.

4

PETER
THE BLACKBIRD

You know that guy who always jokes about starting his shopping at lunchtime on Christmas Eve? Peter is that guy. It potentially goes some way towards explaining why he's never yet found a long-term mate. He's been looking for a while for someone who will laugh with him at his haphazard gifting, which probably has a 50/50 rate of blinding success or crushing failure. He'd be happy to find someone tolerant of the task of earmarking their own gift in early November (and accepting that if they don't select that gift wrapping option they'll have to make a choice between doing it themselves, or finding a box decorated with warehouse barcodes instead of ribbons under the tree!).

BODY/NECK/HEAD

Working in Charcoal

Begin by dc6 into ring

Rnd 1 (dc2 into next st) 6 times (12 sts)

Rnd 2 (dc1, dc2 into next st) 6 times (18)

Rnd 3 (dc2, dc2 into next st) 6 times (24)

Rnd 4 (dc3, dc2 into next st) 6 times (30)

Rnd 5 (dc4, dc2 into next st) 6 times (36)

Rnd 6 (dc5, dc2 into next st) 6 times (42)

Rnds 7-9 dc (3 rnds)

Rnd 10 (dc5, dc2tog) 6 times (36)

Rnds 11-14 dc (4 rnds)

Rnd 15 (dc4, dc2tog) 6 times (30)

Rnds 16-19 dc (4 rnds)

Rnd 20 (dc3, dc2tog) 6 times (24)

Rnd 21 dc

Rnd 22 (dc2tog) 9 times, dc6 (15)

Rnd 23 (dc2tog) 5 times, dc5 (10)

Stuff and continue

Rnd 24 dc

Rnd 25 (dc2 into next st) 10 times (20)

Rnd 26 (dc3, dc2 into next st) 5 times (25)

Rnd 27 (dc4, dc2 into next st) 5 times (30)

Rnd 28 (dc2, dc2 into next st) 10 times (40)

Rnds 29-31 dc (3 rnds)

Rnd 32 (dc8, dc2tog) 4 times (36)

Rnd 33 dc

Rnd 34 (dc4, dc2tog) 6 times (30)

Rnd 35 (dc3, dc2tog) 6 times (24)

Rnd 36 (dc2, dc2tog) 6 times (18)

Rnd 37 dc

Rnd 38 (dc2tog) 9 times (9)

Rnd 39 (dc1, dc2tog) 3 times (6)

LEGS (make two)

Working in Charcoal

Ch12 and sl st to join into a circle

Rnds 1-3 dc (3 rnds)

Rnd 4 (dc2, dc2tog) 3 times (9)

Rnd 5 (dc1, dc2tog) 3 times (6)

Change to Yellow

Rnds 6-12 dc (7 rnds)

Rnd 13 (dc2 into next st) 6 times (12)

Rnds 14-15 dc (2 rnds)

Rnd 16 (dc2tog) 6 times (6)

Rnds 17-24 dc (8 rnds)

Rnd 25 (dc2 into next st) 6 times (12)

Rnd 26 (dc1, dc2 into next st) 6 times (18)

Split into three rnds of 6 sts and work each as follows:

Rnds 1-3 dc (3 rnds)

Rnd 4 dc2tog, dc4 (5)

Rnds 5-6 dc (2 rnds)

Rnd 7 dc2tog, dc3 (4)

BACK DIGIT (optional)

SLIP STITCH TRAVERSE (see page 19) a 6-st root on
   back of foot and work as follows:

Rnd 1 dc

Rnd 2 dc2tog, dc4 (5)

Rnds 3-4 dc (2 rnds)

Rnd 5 dc2tog, dc3 (4)

Lightly stuff thigh and sew flat across top to close.

WINGS (make two)

Working in Charcoal

Begin by dc6 into ring

Rnd 1 (dc1, dc2 into next st) 3 times (9)

Rnd 2 dc8, dc2 into next st (10)

Rnd 3 dc

Rnd 4 dc9, dc2 into next st (11)

Rnd 5 dc

Rnd 6 dc10, dc2 into next st (12)

Rnd 7 dc

Rnd 8 dc11, dc2 into next st (13)

Rnd 9 dc

Rnd 10 dc12, dc2 into next st (14)

Rnd 11 dc

Rnd 12 (dc6, dc2 into next st) twice (16)

Rnd 13 dc2 into next st, dc14, dc2 into next st (18)

Rnd 14 dc2 into next st, dc16, dc2 into next st (20)

Rnd 15 dc2 into next st, dc18, dc2 into next st (22)

Rnd 16 dc2 into next st, dc20, dc2 into next st (24)

Rnd 17 dc2 into next st, dc22, dc2 into next st (26)

Rnds 18-21 dc (4 rnds)

Rnd 22 (dc11, dc2tog) twice (24)

Rnd 23 (dc2, dc2tog) 6 times (18)

Rnd 24 dc

Rnd 25 (dc1, dc2tog) 6 times (12)

Rnd 26 (dc2tog) 6 times (6)

Do not stuff.

BEAK

Working in Yellow

Ch8 and sl st to join into a circle

Rnd 1 dc

Rnd 2 (dc2, dc2tog) twice (6)

Rnds 3-4 dc (2 rnds)

Rnd 5 (dc1, dc2tog) twice (4)

Rnd 6 (dc2tog) twice (2)

Stuff lightly and sew into position.

TAIL

Working in Charcoal

Ch16 and sl st to join into a circle

Rnds 1-6 dc (6 rnds)

Split into two rnds of 8 sts and work each as follows:

Rnds 1-4 dc (4 rnds)

Rnd 5 dc7, dc2 into next st (9)

Rnds 6-8 dc (3 rnds)

Rnd 9 dc8, dc2 into next st (10)

Rnds 10-12 dc (3 rnds)

Rnd 13 (dc3, dc2tog) twice (8)

Rnd 14 (dc2, dc2tog) twice (6)

Rnd 15 (dc2tog) 3 times (3)

Finish by sewing eyes into place with Black yarn.

15

GILBERT
THE PHEASANT

There's no better time of year to be in a church choir than when you get to swap the hymns for carols, put your Christmas jumper on, and get ready to be jolly. Gilbert's never happier than when he's both eating cake and belting out his 'fa-la-la-la-laaas' as loud as his lungs will allow (and that tends to be for most of the festive period). He spends Christmas fuelled by mince pies, panettone, and Yule logs, moving energetically from one sugar high to the next. Knowing of his fondness for festive puddings, he inherited his late great aunt's handwritten recipe book and, for many years now, he has spent the whole of stir-up Sunday popping sixpences into steaming bowls and humming all his favourite 'pa-rup-a-pum-pums' as he bakes until he drops.

SPOT PATTERN

Work 3 sts Camel, 2 sts Chestnut

BODY/NECK/HEAD

Working in SPOT PATTERN

Begin by dc6 into ring

Rnd 1 (dc2 into next st) 6 times (12 sts)

Rnd 2 (dc1, dc2 into next st) 6 times (18)

Rnd 3 (dc2, dc2 into next st) 6 times (24)

Rnd 4 (dc3, dc2 into next st) 6 times (30)

Rnd 5 (dc4, dc2 into next st) 6 times (36)

Change to Stone

Rnd 6 (dc5, dc2 into next st) 6 times (42)

Rnds 7-9 dc (3 rnds)

Rnd 10 (dc5, dc2tog) 6 times (36)

Rnds 11-14 dc (4 rnds)

Rnd 15 (dc4, dc2tog) 6 times (30)

Change to working odd rnds in SPOT PATTERN and
even rnds as 2 sts Camel, 2 sts Chestnut

Rnds 16-19 dc (4 rnds)

Rnd 20 (dc3, dc2tog) 6 times (24)

Rnd 21 dc

Change to Cream

Rnd 22 (dc2tog) 9 times, dc6 (15)

Rnd 23 (dc2tog) 5 times, dc5 (10)

Change to Green

Rnd 24 dc

Rnd 25 (dc2 into next st) 5 times Orange, (dc2 into next
st) 5 times Green (20)

Rnd 26 (dc3, dc2 into next st) twice, dc2 Orange, dc1,
dc2 into next st, (dc3, dc2 into next st) twice Green (25)

Rnd 27 (dc4, dc2 into next st) twice, dc2 Orange, dc2, dc2
into next st, (dc4, dc2 into next st) twice Green (30)

Rnd 28 (dc2, dc2 into next st) 4 times, dc2 Orange, dc2
into next st, (dc2, dc2 into next st) 5 times Green (40)

Rnds 29-31 dc18 Orange, dc22 Green (3 rnds)

Rnd 32 dc8, dc2tog, dc8 Orange, dc2tog, (dc8, dc2tog)
twice Green (36)

Rnd 33 dc17 Orange, dc19 Green

Rnd 34 (dc4, dc2tog) twice, dc4 Orange, dc2tog across
both colours, (dc4, dc2tog) 3 times Green (30)

Continue in Green

Rnd 35 (dc3, dc2tog) 6 times (24)

Rnd 36 (dc2, dc2tog) 6 times (18)

Rnd 37 dc

Rnd 38 (dc2tog) 9 times (9)

Rnd 39 (dc1, dc2tog) 3 times (6)

LEGS (make two)

Working in Chestnut

Ch12 and sl st to join into a circle

Rnds 1-3 dc (3 rnds)

Rnd 4 (dc2, dc2tog) 3 times (9)

Rnd 5 (dc1, dc2tog) 3 times (6)

Change to Stone

Rnds 6-11 dc (6 rnds)

Rnd 12 (dc2 into next st) 6 times (12)

Rnds 13-14 dc (2 rnds)

Rnd 15 (dc2tog) 6 times (6)

Rnds 16-22 dc (7 rnds)

Rnd 23 (dc2 into next st) 6 times (12)

Rnd 24 (dc1, dc2 into next st) 6 times (18)

Split into three rnds of 6 sts and work each as follows:
Rnds 1-3 dc (3 rnds)
Rnd 4 dc2tog, dc4 (5)
Rnds 5-6 dc (2 rnds)
Rnd 7 dc2tog, dc3 (4)

BACK DIGIT (optional)
SLIP STITCH TRAVERSE (see page 19) a 6-st root on
   back of foot and work as follows:
Rnd 1 dc
Rnd 2 dc2tog, dc4 (5)
Rnds 3-4 dc (2 rnds)
Rnd 5 dc2tog, dc3 (4)
Lightly stuff thigh and sew flat across top to close.

WINGS (make two)
Working in Chestnut
Begin by dc6 into ring
Rnd 1 (dc2 into next st) 6 times (12)
Rnd 2 (dc1, dc2 into next st) 6 times (18)
Rnd 3 (dc2, dc2 into next st) 6 times (24)
Rnds 4-5 dc (2 rnds)
Rnd 6 (dc2, dc2tog) 6 times (18)
Rnds 7-8 dc (2 rnds)
Rnd 9 (dc4, dc2tog) 3 times (15)
Rnd 10 dc
Rnd 11 (dc1, dc2tog) 5 times (10)
Rnds 12-13 dc (2 rnds)
Rnd 14 (dc2tog) 5 times (5)
Do not stuff.

BEAK
Working in Oatmeal
Ch8 and sl st to join into a circle
Rnds 1-2 dc (2 rnds)
Rnd 3 dc6, dc2tog (7)
Rnd 4 dc5, dc2tog (6)
Rnd 5 dc4, dc2tog (5)
Rnd 6 dc
Rnd 7 dc3, dc2tog (4)
Rnd 8 dc2, dc2tog (3)
Stuff lightly and sew into position.

TAIL
Working in Oatmeal with 1 rnd Fudge stripe every
   4th rnd throughout
Ch16 and sl st to join into a circle
Rnds 1-6 dc (6 rnds)
Split into two rnds of 8 sts and work each as follows:
Rnds 1-7 dc (7 rnds)
Rnd 8 dc7, dc2 into next st (9)
Rnds 9-14 dc (6 rnds)
Rnd 15 dc8, dc2 into next st (10)
Rnds 16-18 dc (3 rnds)
Rnd 19 (dc3, dc2tog) twice (8)
Rnd 20 (dc2, dc2tog) twice (6)
Rnd 21 (dc2tog) 3 times (3)
Rnd 22 dc2tog, dc1 (2)
Do not stuff.
Sew into alert position by sewing base of tail flat against
   back of body.

Finish by sewing eyes into place with Black yarn.

6

LYDIA
THE GOOSE

Lydia's feeling anxious this Christmas, but thankfully has very little left to do to feather the nest while she counts down to her due date. Although at first, she was shocked to hear she was expecting her baby on the 25th of December, she's since grown very fond of the idea of a very special present arriving that day. Her mind is filling the hours, rattling through long lists of festive names that might be perfect once she first takes her baby under her wing. With just days to go, this very organised goose already cooked the turkey and all the trimmings last week, and has it all safely in her freezer to ensure that whatever happens she won't miss her Christmas dinner!

BODY/NECK/HEAD

Working in Shale

Begin by dc6 into ring

Rnd 1 (dc2 into next st) 6 times (12 sts)

Rnd 2 (dc1, dc2 into next st) 6 times (18)

Rnd 3 (dc2, dc2 into next st) 6 times (24)

Rnd 4 (dc3, dc2 into next st) 6 times (30)

Rnd 5 (dc4, dc2 into next st) 6 times (36)

Rnd 6 (dc5, dc2 into next st) 6 times (42)

Rnds 7-9 dc (3 rnds)

Rnd 10 (dc5, dc2tog) 6 times (36)

Rnds 11-14 dc (4 rnds)

Rnd 15 (dc4, dc2tog) 6 times (30)

Rnds 16-19 dc (4 rnds)

Rnd 20 (dc3, dc2tog) 6 times (24)

Rnd 21 dc

Rnd 22 (dc2tog) 9 times, dc6 (15)

Rnd 23 (dc2tog) 5 times, dc5 (10)

Stuff and continue

Rnds 24-29 dc (6 rnds)

Rnd 30 (dc2 into next st) 10 times (20)

Rnd 31 (dc3, dc2 into next st) 5 times (25)

Rnd 32 (dc4, dc2 into next st) 5 times (30)

Rnd 33 (dc2, dc2 into next st) 10 times (40)

Rnds 34-36 dc (3 rnds)

Rnd 37 (dc8, dc2tog) 4 times (36)

Rnd 38 dc

Rnd 39 (dc4, dc2tog) 6 times (30)

Rnd 40 (dc3, dc2tog) 6 times (24)

Rnd 41 (dc2, dc2tog) 6 times (18)

Rnd 42 dc

Rnd 43 (dc2tog) 9 times (9)

Rnd 44 (dc1, dc2tog) 3 times (6)

LEGS (make two)

Working in Shale

Ch16 and sl st to join into a circle

Rnds 1-5 dc (5 rnds)

Rnd 6 (dc2, dc2tog) 4 times (12)

Rnd 7 (dc1, dc2tog) 4 times (8)

Change to Orange

Rnds 8-9 dc (2 rnds)

Rnd 10 (dc1, dc2 into next st) 4 times (12)

Rnds 11-12 dc (2 rnds)

Rnd 13 (dc1, dc2tog) 4 times (8)

Rnds 14-20 dc (7 rnds)

Rnd 21 (dc2 into next st) 8 times (16)

Rnd 22 dc

Rnd 23 (dc7, dc2 into next st) twice (18)

Rnd 24 (dc8, dc2 into next st) twice (20)

Rnd 25 dc

Rnd 26 (dc9, dc2 into next st) twice (22)

Rnd 27 dc

Rnd 28 (dc10, dc2 into next st) twice (24)

Rnds 29-31 dc (3 rnds)

Split into three rnds of 8 sts and work each as follows:

Rnd 1 dc

Rnd 2 (dc2tog) 4 times (4)

Rnd 3 (dc2tog) twice (2)

Lightly stuff thigh and sew flat across top to close.

WINGS (make two)

Working in Charcoal

Begin by dc6 into ring

Rnd 1 (dc1, dc2 into next st) 3 times (9)

Rnd 2 dc8, dc2 into next st (10)

Change to Shale

Rnd 3 dc

Rnd 4 dc9, dc2 into next st (11)

Change to Charcoal

Rnd 5 dc

Rnd 6 dc10, dc2 into next st (12)

Change to Shale

Rnd 7 dc

Rnd 8 dc11, dc2 into next st (13)

Change to Charcoal

Rnd 9 dc

Rnd 10 dc12, dc2 into next st (14)

Change to Shale

Rnd 11 dc

Rnd 12 (dc6, dc2 into next st) twice (16)

Rnd 13 dc2 into next st, dc14, dc2 into next st (18)

Change to Charcoal

Rnd 14 dc2 into next st, dc16, dc2 into next st (20)

Change to Shale

Rnd 15 dc2 into next st, dc18, dc2 into next st (22)

Rnd 16 dc2 into next st, dc20, dc2 into next st (24)

Rnd 17 dc2 into next st, dc22, dc2 into next st (26)

Change to Charcoal

Rnd 18 dc

Continue in Shale

Rnds 19-21 dc (3 rnds)

Rnd 22 (dc11, dc2tog) twice (24)

Rnd 23 (dc2, dc2tog) 6 times (18)

Rnd 24 dc

Rnd 25 (dc1, dc2tog) 6 times (12)

Rnd 26 (dc2tog) 6 times (6)

Do not stuff.

BEAK

Working in Orange

Begin by dc6 into ring

Rnd 1 (dc2 into next st) 6 times (12)

Rnd 2 (dc1, dc2 into next st) 6 times (18)

Rnds 3-6 dc (4 rnds)

Rnd 7 (dc7, dc2tog) twice (16)

Rnd 8 dc

Rnd 9 (dc7, dc2 into next st) twice (18)

Rnd 10-13 dc (4 rnds)

Stuff lightly and sew into position.

TAIL

Working in Shale

Ch18 and sl st to join into a circle

Rnds 1-2 dc (2 rnds)

Change to Charcoal

Rnd 3 (dc2, dc2 into next st) 6 times (24)

Change to Shale

Rnd 4 dc

Split into three rnds of 8 sts and work each as follows:

Rnd 1 dc

Change to Charcoal

Rnds 2-4 dc (3 rnds)

Rnd 5 (dc2tog) 4 times (4)

Do not stuff.

Finish by sewing eyes into place with Black yarn.

7

MARGOT

THE SWAN

Margot has been persuaded out of retirement to don her tutu one last time this Christmas. As a fundraiser for a high-profile charity, she'll perform her pirouetting finale in a star-studded performance of The Nutcracker. Masking any hints of arthritis as she retakes the spotlight after decades, she's channelling her teenage self as she prepares to play the first role she wore her pointe shoes on stage for. For once her poised and steely guard is down as she rehearses to again plié with the Mouse King with the memories of over five decades of watching other sugar plum fairies spinning around inside her mind.

═══════════════════════════════════

BODY/NECK/HEAD

Working in Cream

Begin by dc6 into ring

Rnd 1 (dc2 into next st) 6 times (12 sts)

Rnd 2 (dc1, dc2 into next st) 6 times (18)

Rnd 3 (dc2, dc2 into next st) 6 times (24)

Rnd 4 (dc3, dc2 into next st) 6 times (30)

Rnd 5 (dc4, dc2 into next st) 6 times (36)

Rnd 6 (dc5, dc2 into next st) 6 times (42)

Rnds 7-9 dc (3 rnds)

Rnd 10 (dc5, dc2tog) 6 times (36)

Rnds 11-14 dc (4 rnds)

Rnd 15 (dc4, dc2tog) 6 times (30)

Rnds 16-19 dc (4 rnds)

Rnd 20 (dc3, dc2tog) 6 times (24)

Rnd 21 dc

Rnd 22 (dc2tog) 9 times, dc 6 (15)

Rnd 23 (dc2tog) 5 times, dc 5 (10)

Rnds 24-29 dc (6 rnds)

Rnd 30 (dc2 into next st) 10 times (20)

Rnd 31 (dc3, dc2 into next) 5 times (25)

Rnd 32 (dc4, dc2 into next) 5 times (30)

Rnd 33 (dc2, dc2 into next) 10 times (40)

Rnds 34-36 dc (3 rnds)

Rnd 37 (dc8, dc2tog) 4 times (36)

Rnd 38 dc

Rnd 39 (dc4, dc2tog) 6 times (30)

Rnd 40 (dc3, dc2tog) 6 times (24)

Rnd 41 (dc2, dc2tog) 6 times (18)

Rnd 42 dc

Rnd 43 (dc2tog) 9 times (9)

Rnd 44 (dc1, dc2tog) 3 times (6)

LEGS (make two)

Working in Cream

Ch15 and sl st to join into a circle

Rnds 1-2 dc (2 rnds)

Rnd 3 (dc3, dc2tog) 3 times (12)

Rnd 4 (dc2, dc2tog) 3 times (9)

Rnds 5-6 dc (2 rnds)

Rnd 7 (dc1, dc2tog) 3 times (6)

Change to Black

Rnds 8-12 dc (5 rnds)

Rnd 13 (dc2 into next st) 6 times (12)

Rnds 14-15 dc (2 rnds)

Rnd 16 (dc2tog) 6 times (6)

Rnds 17-22 dc (6 rnds)

Rnd 23 (dc2 into next st) 6 times (12)

Rnd 24 dc

Rnd 25 (dc5, dc2 into next st) twice (14)

Rnd 26 (dc6, dc2 into next st) twice (16)

Rnd 27 (dc7, dc2 into next st) twice (18)

Rnds 28-32 dc (5 rnds)

Split into three rnds of 6 sts and work each as follows:

Rnd 1 dc

Rnd 2 (dc2tog) 3 times (3)

Lightly stuff thigh and sew flat across top to close.

WINGS (make two)

Working in Cream

Begin by dc6 into ring

Rnd 1 (dc2 into next st) 6 times (12)

Rnd 2 (dc1, dc2 into next st) 6 times (18)
Rnd 3 (dc2, dc2 into next st) 6 times (24)
Rnd 4 (dc3, dc2 into next st) 6 times (30)
Rnds 5-10 dc (6 rnds)
Split 10 sts and work as follows:
Rnds 1-4 dc (4 rnds)
Rnd 5 (dc2tog) 5 times (5)
Rejoin and work remaining 20 sts as follows:
Rnds 1-3 dc (3 rnds)
Rnd 4 dc5 (incomplete rnd)
Split into two rnds of 10 sts and work first 10-st rnd as
follows:
Rnds 1-4 dc (4 rnds)
Rnd 5 (dc2tog) 5 times (5)
Rejoin and work final 10-st rnd as follows:
Rnds 1-6 dc (6 rnds)
Rnd 7 (dc2tog) 5 times (5)
Do not stuff.

BEAK

Working in Black
Begin by dc6 into ring
Change to Orange
Rnd 1 (dc2 into next st) 6 times (12)
Rnd 2 (dc1, dc2 into next st) 6 times (18)
Rnds 3-5 dc (3 rnds)
Rnd 6 (dc4, dc2tog) 3 times (15)
Rnds 7-12 dc (6 rnds)
Change to Black
Rnd 13 (dc4, dc2 into next st) 3 times (18)
Rnds 14-15 dc (2 rnds)
Rnd 16 (dc2, dc2 into next st) 6 times (24)
Stuff lightly and sew into position

TAIL

Working in Cream
Ch18 and sl st to join into a circle
Rnd 1 dc
Rnd 2 (dc2, dc2 into next st) 6 times (24)
Rnd 3 (dc5, dc2 into next st) 4 times (28)
Split into three rnds with one rnd of 12 sts in the middle
and two rnds of 8 sts either side
Work each 8-st rnd as follows:
Rnds 1-2 dc (2 rnds)
Rnd 3 (dc2tog) 4 times (4)
Rejoin and work the central 12-st rnd as follows:
Rnds 1-4 dc (4 rnds)
Rnd 5 (dc2, dc2tog) 3 times (9)
Rnd 6 (dc1, dc2tog) 3 times (6)
Rnd 7 (dc2tog) 3 times (3)
Do not stuff.

Finish by sewing eyes into place with Black yarn.

8

DELILAH
THE CATTLE EGRET

Known as somewhat of an eccentric throughout the entire village she lives in, Delilah is planning on really living up to her reputation this Christmas. She's embarking upon a culinary experiment of cooking the roast turkey on her award-winning shiny, new barbecue. Dissatisfied with the drizzly, underwhelming summer this year, she only scraped half a dozen chances to incinerate a few blocks of halloumi, and so is desperate to turn her skills to something more challenging. With military precision she's meticulously calculated timings, temperatures and seasoning, which she's confident will land dinner on the table at the perfect time for a morning stretch of the legs and a post-dinner snooze in front of the TV.

BODY/NECK/HEAD

Working in Cream

Begin by dc6 into ring

Rnd 1 (dc2 into next st) 6 times (12 sts)

Rnd 2 (dc1, dc2 into next st) 6 times (18)

Rnd 3 (dc2, dc2 into next st) 6 times (24)

Rnd 4 (dc3, dc2 into next st) 6 times (30)

Rnd 5 (dc4, dc2 into next st) 6 times (36)

Rnd 6 (dc5, dc2 into next st) 6 times (42)

Rnds 7-9 dc (3 rnds)

Rnd 10 (dc5, dc2tog) 6 times (36)

Rnds 11-14 dc (4 rnds)

Rnd 15 (dc4, dc2tog) 6 times (30)

Rnds 16-19 dc (4 rnds)

Rnd 20 (dc3, dc2tog) 6 times (24)

Rnd 21 dc

Rnd 22 (dc2tog) 9 times, dc6 (15)

Rnd 23 (dc2tog) 5 times, dc5 (10)

Stuff and continue

Rnds 24-29 dc (6 rnds)

Rnd 30 (dc2 into next st) 10 times (20)

Rnd 31 (dc3, dc2 into next st) 5 times (25)

Work 2cm LOOP STITCH (see page 17) every st
   as instructed

Rnd 32 dc4, dc2 into next st, dc4 loop, dc2 into next st
   loop, (dc4, dc2 into next st) 3 times (30)

Rnd 33 (dc2, dc2 into next st) twice, (dc2 loop, dc2 into
   next st loop) twice, (dc2, dc2 into next st) 6 times (40)

Continue without loops

Rnds 34-36 dc (3 rnds)

Rnd 37 (dc8, dc2tog) 4 times (36)

Rnd 38 dc

Rnd 39 (dc4, dc2tog) 6 times (30)

Rnd 40 (dc3, dc2tog) 6 times (24)

Rnd 41 (dc2, dc2tog) 6 times (18)

Rnd 42 dc

Rnd 43 (dc2tog) 9 times (9)

Rnd 44 (dc1, dc2tog) 3 times (6)

LEGS (make two)

Working in Cream

Ch12 and sl st to join into a circle

Rnds 1-3 dc (3 rnds)

Rnd 4 (dc2, dc2tog) 3 times (9)

Rnd 5 (dc1, dc2tog) 3 times (6)

Change to Yellow

Rnds 6-14 dc (9 rnds)

Change to Charcoal

Rnd 15 (dc2 into next st) 6 times (12)

Rnds 16-17 dc (2 rnds)

Rnd 18 (dc2tog) 6 times (6)

Rnds 19-28 dc (10 rnds)

Rnd 29 (dc2 into next st) 6 times (12)

Rnd 30 (dc1, dc2 into next st) 6 times (18)

Split into three rnds of 6 sts and work each as follows:

Rnds 1-4 dc (4 rnds)

Rnd 5 dc2tog, dc4 (5)

Rnds 6-7 dc (2 rnds)

Rnd 8 dc2tog, dc3 (4)

Rnd 9 (dc2tog) twice (2)

BACK DIGIT (optional)

SLIP STITCH TRAVERSE (see page 19) a 6-st root on
  the back of the foot and work as follows:

Rnds 1-2 dc (2 rnds)

Rnd 3 (dc2tog) 3 times (3)

Lightly stuff thigh and sew flat across top to close.

WINGS (make two)

Working in Cream

Begin by dc6 into ring

Rnd 1 (dc1, dc2 into next st) 3 times (9)

Rnd 2 dc8, dc2 into next st (10)

Rnd 3 dc

Rnd 4 dc9, dc2 into next st (11)

Rnd 5 dc

Rnd 6 dc10, dc2 into next st (12)

Rnd 7 dc

Rnd 8 dc11, dc2 into next st (13)

Rnd 9 dc

Rnd 10 dc12, dc2 into next st (14)

Rnd 11 dc

Rnd 12 (dc6, dc2 into next st) twice (16)

Rnd 13 dc2 into next st, dc14, dc2 into next st (18)

Rnd 14 dc2 into next st, dc16, dc2 into next st (20)

Rnd 15 dc2 into next st, dc18, dc2 into next st (22)

Rnd 16 dc2 into next st, dc20, dc2 into next st (24)

Rnd 17 dc2 into next st, dc22, dc2 into next st (26)

Rnds 18-21 dc (4 rnds)

Rnd 22 (dc11, dc2tog) twice (24)

Rnd 23 (dc2, dc2tog) 6 times (18)

Rnd 24 dc

Rnd 25 (dc1, dc2tog) 6 times (12)

Rnd 26 (dc2tog) 6 times (6)

BEAK

Working in Yellow

Ch15 and sl st to join into a circle

Rnds 1-5 dc (5 rnds)

Rnd 6 (dc3, dc2tog) 3 times (12)

Rnds 7-9 dc (3 rnds)

Rnd 10 (dc2, dc2tog) 3 times (9)

Change to Charcoal

Rnds 11-13 dc (3 rnds)

Rnd 14 (dc1, dc2tog) 3 times (6)

Stuff lightly and sew into position.

EYES (make two)

Working in Yellow

Begin by dc6 in ring

Sew into position.

TAIL

Working in Cream

Ch18 and sl st to join into a circle

Rnds 1-3 dc (3 rnds)

Rnd 4 (dc2, dc2 into next st) 6 times (24)

Rnd 5 dc

Split into three rnds of 8 sts and work each as follows:

Rnds 1-7 dc (7 rnds)

Rnd 8 (dc2, dc2tog) twice (6)

Rnd 9 (dc2tog) 3 times (3)

Do not stuff.

Finish by sewing eyes into place with Black yarn.

9

LOIS
THE GREAT CORMORANT

Lois has woken up with regrets following one too many at her office party last night. Quite predictably, once the bubbles started pouring and she started rocking around the Christmas tree, her sensible plan to just have one and then drive herself home went out the window. She surprised herself with her dominance on the dancefloor this year, waddling out all her best moves once the disco tunes replaced the Christmas party mix. Dragging herself into a boiling hot shower she wonders: Why didn't she eat more canapés? Was the last song of the night really THAT track? Why did she decide to share the taxi home? Does she really now have to go and get the bus? Who knows what gossip she might face around the coffee machine at elevenses...

BODY/NECK/HEAD

Working in Charcoal

Begin by dc6 into ring

Rnd 1 (dc2 into next st) 6 times (12 sts)

Rnd 2 (dc1, dc2 into next st) 6 times (18)

Rnd 3 (dc2, dc2 into next st) 6 times (24)

Rnd 4 (dc3, dc2 into next st) 6 times (30)

Rnd 5 (dc4, dc2 into next st) 6 times (36)

Rnd 6 (dc5, dc2 into next st) 6 times (42)

Rnds 7-9 dc (3 rnds)

Rnd 10 (dc5, dc2tog) 6 times (36)

Rnds 11-14 dc (4 rnds)

Rnd 15 (dc4, dc2tog) 6 times (30)

Rnds 16-19 dc (4 rnds)

Rnd 20 (dc3, dc2tog) 6 times (24)

Rnd 21 dc

Rnd 22 (dc2tog) 9 times, dc6 (15)

Rnd 23 (dc2tog) 5 times, dc5 (10)

Stuff and continue

Rnds 24-28 dc (5 rnds)

Rnd 29 (dc2 into next st) 10 times (20)

Rnd 30 (dc3, dc2 into next st) 5 times (25)

Rnd 31 (dc4, dc2 into next st) 5 times (30)

Rnd 32 (dc2, dc2 into next st) 10 times (40)

Rnds 33-35 dc5 Charcoal, dc5 Cream, dc10 Yellow, dc5 Cream, dc15 Charcoal (3 rnds)

Rnd 36 dc5 Charcoal, dc3, dc2tog Cream, dc8, dc2tog Yellow, dc5 Cream, dc3, dc2tog, dc8, dc2tog Charcoal (36)

Rnd 37 dc5 Charcoal, dc4 Cream, dc9 Yellow, dc5 Cream, dc13 Charcoal

Continue in Charcoal

Rnd 38 (dc4, dc2tog) 6 times (30)

Rnd 39 (dc3, dc2tog) 6 times (24)

Rnd 40 (dc2, dc2tog) 6 times (18)

Rnd 41 dc

Rnd 42 (dc2tog) 9 times (9)

Rnd 43 (dc1, dc2tog) 3 times (6)

LEGS (make two)

Working in Cream

Ch16 and sl st to join into a circle

Rnds 1-5 dc (5 rnds)

Rnd 6 (dc2, dc2tog) 4 times (12)

Rnd 7 (dc1, dc2tog) 4 times (8)

Change to Charcoal

Rnds 8-9 dc (2 rnds)

Rnd 10 (dc1, dc2 into next st) 4 times (12)

Rnds 11-12 dc (2 rnds)

Rnd 13 (dc1, dc2tog) 4 times (8)

Rnds 14-20 dc (7 rnds)

Rnd 21 (dc2 into next st) 8 times (16)

Rnd 22 dc

Rnd 23 (dc7, dc2 into next st) twice (18)

Rnd 24 (dc8, dc2 into next st) twice (20)

Rnd 25 dc

Rnd 26 (dc9, dc2 into next st) twice (22)

Rnd 27 dc

Rnd 28 (dc10, dc2 into next st) twice (24)

Rnds 29-31 dc (3 rnds)

Split into three rnds of 8 sts and work each as follows:

Rnd 1 dc

Rnd 2 (dc2tog) 4 times (4)
Rnd 3 (dc2tog) twice (2)

BACK DIGIT (optional)
SLIP STITCH TRAVERSE (see page 19) a 6-st root
    on back of foot and work as follows:
Rnd 1 dc
Rnd 2 dc2tog, dc4 (5)
Rnd 3 dc
Rnd 4 dc2tog, dc3 (4)
Lightly stuff thigh and sew flat across top to close.

WINGS (make two)
Working in Charcoal
Begin by dc6 into ring
Rnd 1 (dc1, dc2 into next st) 3 times (9)
Rnd 2 dc8, dc2 into next st (10)
Rnd 3 dc
Rnd 4 dc9, dc2 into next st (11)
Rnd 5 dc
Rnd 6 dc10, dc2 into next st (12)
Rnd 7 dc
Rnd 8 dc11, dc2 into next st (13)
Rnd 9 dc
Rnd 10 dc12, dc2 into next st (14)
Rnd 11 dc
Rnd 12 (dc6, dc2 into next st) twice (16)
Rnd 13 dc2 into next st, dc14, dc2 into next st (18)
Rnd 14 dc2 into next st, dc16, dc2 into next st (20)
Rnd 15 dc2 into next st, dc18, dc2 into next st (22)
Rnd 16 dc2 into next st, dc20, dc2 into next st (24)
Rnd 17 dc2 into next st, dc22, dc2 into next st (26)
Rnds 18-21 dc (4 rnds)

Rnd 22 (dc11, dc2tog) twice (24)
Rnd 23 (dc2, dc2tog) 6 times (18)
Rnd 24 dc
Rnd 25 (dc1, dc2tog) 6 times (12)
Rnd 26 (dc2tog) 6 times (6)
Do not stuff.

BEAK
Working in Oatmeal
Ch15 and sl st to join into a circle
Rnds 1-8 dc (8 rnds)
Rnd 9 (dc3, dc2tog) 3 times (12)
Rnds 10-12 dc (3 rnds)
Rnd 13 (dc2, dc2tog) 3 times (9)
Rnd 14 dc
Rnd 15 (dc1, dc2tog) 3 times (6)
Stuff lightly and sew into position.

TAIL
Working in Charcoal
Ch18 and sl st to join into a circle
Rnds 1-3 dc (3 rnds)
Rnd 4 (dc2, dc2 into next st) 6 times (24)
Rnd 5 dc
Split into three rnds of 8 sts and work each as follows:
Rnds 1-6 dc (6 rnds)
Rnd 7 dc2 into next st, dc7 (9)
Rnds 8-11 dc (4 rnds)
Rnd 12 (dc1, dc2tog) 3 times (6)
Do not stuff.

Finish by sewing eyes into place with Black yarn.

10

AGNES
THE HERON

It was the night before Christmas and Agnes flopped down onto the middle of her sofa and crossed her long legs as she put her feet up on the coffee table. We all know that the festive season can be a busy time, but this year Agnes certainly deserves far more than a lump of coal in her stocking. Between school nativity plays, shopping lists, endless 'get-togethers' and very hard logistics planning to get all her elderly relatives in the right place for tonight, she is feeling frazzled. Resting her head back on the sofa and closing her eyes just for a second, she takes a long deep breath, enjoys a moment of silence and smiles when she thinks about the children's faces in the morning.

BODY/NECK/HEAD

Working in Silver

Begin by dc6 into ring

Rnd 1 (dc2 into next st) 6 times (12 sts)

Rnd 2 (dc1, dc2 into next st) 6 times (18)

Rnd 3 (dc2, dc2 into next st) 6 times (24)

Rnd 4 (dc3, dc2 into next st) 6 times (30)

Rnd 5 (dc4, dc2 into next st) 6 times (36)

Rnd 6 (dc5, dc2 into next st) 6 times (42)

Rnds 7-9 dc (3 rnds)

Rnd 10 (dc5, dc2tog) 6 times (36)

Rnds 11-14 dc (4 rnds)

Rnd 15 (dc4, dc2tog) 6 times (30)

Rnds 16-19 dc (4 rnds)

Rnd 20 (dc3, dc2tog) 6 times (24)

Rnd 21 dc

Rnd 22 (dc2tog) 9 times, dc6 (15)

Rnd 23 (dc2tog) 5 times, dc5 (10)

Change to Cream

Rnds 24-31 dc (8 rnds)

Rnd 32 (dc2 into next st) 10 times (20)

Rnd 33 (dc3, dc2 into next st) 5 times (25)

Rnd 34 (dc4, dc2 into next st) 5 times (30)

Rnd 35 (dc2, dc2 into next st) 10 times (40)

Rnds 36-38 dc (3 rnds)

Rnd 39 (dc8, dc2tog) 4 times (36)

Rnd 40 dc

Rnd 41 (dc4, dc2tog) 6 times (30)

Rnd 42 (dc3, dc2tog) 6 times (24)

Rnd 43 (dc2, dc2tog) 6 times (18)

Rnd 44 dc

Rnd 45 (dc2tog) 9 times (9)

Rnd 46 (dc1, dc2tog) 3 times (6)

LEGS (make two)

Working in Silver

Ch12 and sl st to join into a circle

Rnds 1-3 dc (3 rnds)

Rnd 4 (dc2, dc2tog) 3 times (9)

Rnd 5 (dc1, dc2tog) 3 times (6)

Change to Oatmeal

Rnds 6-14 dc (9 rnds)

Rnd 15 (dc2 into next st) 6 times (12)

Rnds 16-17 dc (2 rnds)

Rnd 18 (dc2tog) 6 times (6)

Rnds 19-28 dc (10 rnds)

Rnd 29 (dc2 into next st) 6 times (12)

Rnd 30 (dc1, dc2 into next st) 6 times (18)

Split into three rounds of 6 sts and work each as follows:

Rnds 1-4 dc (4 rnds)

Rnd 5 dc2tog, dc4 (5)

Rnds 6-7 dc (2 rnds)

Rnd 8 dc2tog, dc3 (4)

Rnd 9 (dc2tog) twice (2)

Lightly stuff thigh.

BACK DIGIT (optional)

SLIP STITCH TRAVERSE (see page 19) a 6-st root on back of foot and work as follows:

Rnds 1-2 dc (2 rnds)

Rnd 3 (dc2tog) 3 times (3)

WINGS (make two)

Working in Silver

Begin by dc6 into ring

Rnd 1 (dc1, dc2 into next st) 3 times (9)

Rnd 2 dc8, dc2 into next st (10)

Rnd 3 dc

Rnd 4 dc9, dc2 into next st (11)

Rnd 5 dc

Rnd 6 dc10, dc2 into next st (12)

Rnd 7 dc

Rnd 8 dc11, dc2 into next st (13)

Rnd 9 dc

Rnd 10 dc12, dc2 into next st (14)

Rnd 11 dc

Rnd 12 (dc6, dc2 into next st) twice (16)

Rnd 13 dc2 into next st, dc14, dc2 into next st (18)

Rnd 14 dc2 into next st, dc16, dc2 into next st (20)

Rnd 15 dc2 into next st, dc18, dc2 into next st (22)

Rnd 16 dc2 into next st, dc20, dc2 into next st (24)

Rnd 17 dc2 into next st, dc22, dc2 into next st (26)

Rnds 18-21 dc (4 rnds)

Rnd 22 (dc11, dc2tog) twice (24)

Rnd 23 (dc2, dc2tog) 6 times (18)

Rnd 24 dc

Rnd 25 (dc1, dc2tog) 6 times (12)

Rnd 26 (dc2tog) 6 times (6)

Do not stuff.

BEAK

Working in Camel

Ch18 and sl st to join into a circle

Rnds 1-4 dc (4 rnds)

Rnd 5 (dc4, dc2tog) 3 times (15)

Rnds 6-8 dc (3 rnds)

Rnd 9 (dc3, dc2tog) 3 times (12)

Rnds 10-11 dc (2 rnds)

Rnd 12 (dc2, dc2tog) 3 times (9)

Rnds 13-14 dc (2 rnds)

Rnd 15 (dc1, dc2tog) 3 times (6)

Stuff lightly and sew into position.

TAIL

Working in Silver

Ch18 and sl st to join into circle

Rnds 1-2 dc (2 rnds)

Rnd 3 (dc2, dc2 into next st) 6 times (24)

Rnd 4 dc

Change to Black

Split into three rnds of 8 sts and work each as follows:

Rnds 1-4 dc (4 rnds)

Rnd 5 (dc2tog) 4 times (4)

CREST

Working in Black

SLIP STITCH TRAVERSE (see page 18) 8 sts from front
  of head to back, then work one ch18 SLIP STITCH
  CHAIN (see page 19). Repeat on opposite side of head.

Finish by sewing eyes into place with Black yarn.

11

NINA
THE SPOON-BILLED SANDPIPER

Nina is counting down the last few hours at work until she can throw an armful of clothes onto the back seat of her hatchback and hit the long road home for Christmas. Although reluctant to ever admit it, she's been more than just a little homesick these last few months and is longing for some of her Mum's cooking, the smell of freshly laundered sheets and the early-morning cup of tea that appears at her bedside at exactly the right temperature as she opens her eyes. Her first term at university has been a little different to what she had expected, and for the first time ever she's actually looking forward to topping up her dinner plate with veg (and might go as far as to enjoy a couple of sprouts!).

BODY/NECK/HEAD

Working in Cream

Begin by dc6 into ring

Rnd 1 (dc2 into next st) 6 times (12 sts)

Rnd 2 (dc1, dc2 into next st) 6 times (18)

Rnd 3 (dc2, dc2 into next st) 6 times (24)

Rnd 4 (dc3, dc2 into next st) 6 times (30)

Rnd 5 (dc4, dc2 into next st) 6 times (36)

Rnd 6 (dc5, dc2 into next st) 6 times (42)

Rnds 7-9 dc (3 rnds)

Rnd 10 (dc5, dc2tog) 6 times (36)

Rnds 11-14 dc (4 rnds)

Rnd 15 (dc4, dc2tog) 6 times (30)

Rnds 16-19 dc (4 rnds)

Rnd 20 (dc3, dc2tog) 6 times (24)

Rnd 21 dc

Rnd 22 (dc2tog) 9 times, dc6 (15)

Rnd 23 (dc2tog) 5 times, dc5 (10)

Stuff and continue

Rnd 24 dc

Rnd 25 (dc2 into next st) 10 times (20)

Rnd 26 (dc3, dc2 into next st) 5 times (25)

Rnd 27 (dc4, dc2 into next st) 5 times (30)

Rnd 28 (dc2, dc2 into next st) 10 times (40)

Rnds 29-31 dc (3 rnds)

Rnd 32 (dc8, dc2tog) 4 times (36)

Rnd 33 dc

Change to Stone

Rnd 34 (dc4, dc2tog) 6 times (30)

Continue in Stone with every 4th st in Chestnut

Rnd 35 (dc3, dc2tog) 6 times (24)

Rnd 36 (dc2, dc2tog) 6 times (18)

Rnd 37 dc

Rnd 38 (dc2tog) 9 times (9)

Rnd 39 (dc1, dc2tog) 3 times (6)

LEGS (make two)

Working in Cream

Ch12 and sl st to join into a circle

Rnds 1-3 dc (3 rnds)

Rnd 4 (dc2, dc2tog) 3 times (9)

Rnd 5 (dc1, dc2tog) 3 times (6)

Change to Chestnut

Rnds 6-12 dc (7 rnds)

Rnd 13 (dc2 into next st) 6 times (12)

Rnds 14-15 dc (2 rnds)

Rnd 16 (dc2tog) 6 times (6)

Rnds 17-24 dc (8 rnds)

Rnd 25 (dc2 into next st) 6 times (12)

Rnd 26 (dc1, dc2 into next st) 6 times (18)

Split into three rnds of 6 sts and work each as follows:

Rnds 1-5 dc (5 rnds)

Rnd 6 dc2tog, dc4 (5)

Rnds 7-8 dc (2 rnds)

Rnd 9 dc2tog, dc3 (4)

BACK DIGIT (optional)

SLIP STITCH TRAVERSE (see page 19) a 6-st root on the back of the foot and work as follows:

Rnds 1-4 dc (4 rnds)

Rnd 5 (dc2tog) 3 times (3)

Lightly stuff thigh and sew flat across top to close.

WINGS (make two)
Working in Stone with every 4th st in Chestnut
Begin by dc6 into ring
Rnd 1 (dc1, dc2 into next st) 3 times (9)
Rnd 2 dc8, dc2 into next st (10)
Rnd 3 dc
Rnd 4 dc9, dc2 into next st (11)
Rnd 5 dc
Rnd 6 dc10, dc2 into next st (12)
Rnd 7 dc
Rnd 8 dc11, dc2 into next st (13)
Rnd 9 dc
Rnd 10 dc12, dc2 into next st (14)
Rnd 11 dc
Rnd 12 (dc6, dc2 into next st) twice (16)
Rnd 13 dc2 into next st, dc14, dc2 into next st (18)
Rnd 14 dc2 into next st, dc16, dc2 into next st (20)
Rnd 15 dc2 into next st, dc18, dc2 into next st (22)
Rnd 16 dc2 into next st, dc20, dc2 into next st (24)
Rnd 17 dc2 into next st, dc22, dc2 into next st (26)
Rnds 18-21 dc (4 rnds)
Rnd 22 (dc11, dc2tog) twice (24)
Rnd 23 (dc2, dc2tog) 6 times (18)
Rnd 24 dc
Rnd 25 (dc1, dc2tog) 6 times (12)
Rnd 26 (dc2tog) 6 times (6)
Do not stuff.

BEAK
Working in Chestnut
Begin by dc6 into ring
Rnd 1 (dc2 into next st) 6 times (12)
Rnds 2-4 dc (3 rnds)
Rnd 5 (dc1, dc2tog) 4 times (8)
Rnds 6-13 dc (8 rnds)
Rnd 14 (dc3, dc2 into next st) twice (10)
Rnd 15 (dc4, dc2 into next st) twice (12)
Stuff top section lightly and sew flat into position.

TAIL
Working in Cream
Ch16 and sl st to join into a circle
Change to Stone with every 4th st on even rnds in Chestnut
Rnds 1-6 dc (6 rnds)
Split into two rnds of 8 sts and work each as follows:
Rnds 1-4 dc (4 rnds)
Rnd 5 dc7, dc2 into next st (9)
Rnds 6-7 dc (2 rnds)
Rnd 8 dc8, dc2 into next st (10)
Rnds 9-10 dc (2 rnds)
Continue in Chestnut
Rnd 11 (dc4, dc2 into next st) twice (12)
Rnds 12-13 dc (2 rnds)
Rnd 14 (dc2tog) 6 times (6)
Do not stuff.

Finish by sewing eyes into place with Black yarn.

12

JOHN
THE SPOTTED WOODPECKER

Christmas is a very serious business when you live in the UK's number one 'festive postcode' On the stroke of midnight on the 30th November, John has the pleasure of twisting the last twinkling bulb into place and over two hundred thousand flashing lights start to spread cheer to everyone who sees them. It all started when he moved next door to his now best pal Dave, and they had a chat over the fence about plans for putting a few lights in the hedge between their houses. It rapidly became apparent that he'd opportunely moved to a street full of people just as enthusiastic about LEDs as he is, and a couple of years, and miles and miles of fairy lights, later they were attracting visitors from across the county. Every year, just before the twelfth night (and not a moment too soon), they come back down, and he returns to a frugal lifestyle as he spends a year saving to afford the electricity bill for next December!

BODY/NECK/HEAD

Work as Spoonbill BODY (page 85) starting in Ruby and
   changing to Cream after rnd 7 then to Black after 24

Rnd 25 (dc2 into next st) 10 times (20)

Rnd 26 (dc3, dc2 into next st) 5 times (25)

Rnd 27 (dc4, dc2 into next st) 5 times (30)

Rnd 28 (dc2, dc2 into next st) 5 times Ruby, (dc2, dc2
   into next st) 5 times Cream (40)

Rnd 29-31 dc20 Ruby, dc20 Cream (3 rnds)

Rnd 32 (dc8, dc2tog) twice Ruby, (dc8, dc2tog) twice
   Cream (36)

Rnd 33 dc18 Ruby, dc18 Cream

Rnd 34 (dc4, dc2tog) 3 times Ruby, (dc4, dc2tog)
   3 times Cream (30)

Change to Black

Rnd 35 (dc3, dc2tog) 6 times (24) **Rnd 36** (dc2, dc2tog)
   6 times (18) **Rnd 37** dc

Rnd 38 (dc2tog) 9 times (9)

Rnd 39 (dc1, dc2tog) 3 times (6)

LEGS (make two)

Working in Ruby

Ch12 and sl st to join into a circle

Change to Cream

Rnds 1-8 dc (8 rnds)

Rnd 9 (dc2tog) 6 times (6)

Change to Steel

Rnds 10-18 dc (9 rnds)

Next, ch6 and sl st halfway across to other side of rnd to
   form two 8-st rnds (2 from rnd, 6 on chain) Work each
   rnd as follows:

Rnd 1 dc (8)

Rnd 2 (dc1, dc2 into next st) 4 times (12)

Split into two rnds of 6 sts and work each as follows: Rnds
   1-4 dc (4 rnds)

Rnd 5 (dc2, dc2 into next st) twice (8) Rnds 6-7 dc (2 rnds)

Rnd 8 (dc2, dc2tog) twice (6)

Rnd 9 (dc1, dc2tog) twice (4)

Rnd 10 (dc2tog) twice (2)

Lightly stuff thigh and sew flat across top to close.

RIGHT WING

Working in Black

Begin by dc6 into ring

Rnd 1 (dc1, dc2 into next st) 3 times (9)

Change to Cream

Rnd 2 dc8, dc2 into next st (10)

Rnd 3 dc

Change to Black

Rnd 4 dc9, dc2 into next st (11)

Rnd 5 dc

Change to Cream

Rnd 6 dc10, dc2 into next st (12)

Rnd 7 dc

Change to Black

Rnd 8 dc11, dc2 into next st (13)

Rnd 9 dc

Rnd 10 dc7 Black, dc4 Cream, dc1, dc2 into next st
   Black (14)

Rnd 11 dc7 Black, dc4 Cream, dc3 Black

Rnd 12 dc6, dc2 into next st Black, dc4 Cream, dc2, dc2
   into next st Black (16)

Rnd 13 dc2 into next st, dc7 Black, dc4 Cream dc3, dc2 into next st Black (18)

Rnd 14 dc2 into next st, dc8 Black, dc4 Cream, dc4, dc2 into next st Black (20)

Rnd 15 dc2 into next st, dc9 Black, dc4 Cream, dc5, dc2 into next st Black (22)

Rnd 16 dc2 into next st, dc10 Black, dc4 Cream dc6, dc2 into next st Black (24)

Rnd 17 dc2 into next st, dc11 Black, dc4 Cream, dc7, dc2 into next st Black (26)

Rnds 18-22 dc13 Black, dc4 Cream, dc9 Black (5 rnds

Change to Black

Rnd 23 (dc11, dc2tog) twice (24)

Rnd 24 (dc2, dc2tog) 6 times (18)

Change to Cream

Rnd 25 dc

Rnd 26 (dc1, dc2tog) 6 times (12) Rnd 27 (dc2tog) 6 times (6)

Do not stuff.

LEFT WING

Work as Right Wing until:

Rnd 10 dc2 Black, dc4 Cream, dc6, dc2 into next st Black (14)

Rnd 11 dc2 Black, dc4 Cream, dc8 Black

Rnd 12 dc2 Black, dc4 Cream, dc2 into next st Black, dc6, dc2 into next st Black (16)

Rnd 13 dc2 into next st, dc1 Black, dc4 Cream dc9, dc2 into next st Black (18)

Rnd 14 dc2 into next st, dc2 Black, dc4 Cream, dc10, dc2 into next st Black (20)

Rnd 15 dc2 into next st, dc3 Black, dc4 Cream, dc11, dc2 into next st Black (22)

Rnd 16 dc2 into next st, dc4 Black, dc4 Cream dc12, dc2 into next st Black (24)

Rnd 17 dc2 into next st, dc5 Black, dc4 Cream, dc13, dc2 into next st Black (26)

Rnds 18-22 dc7 Black, dc4 Cream, dc15 Black (5 rnds
Continue as Right Wing

BEAK

Working in Steel

Ch12 and sl st to join into a circle

Rnds 1-6 dc (6 rnds)

Rnd 7 (dc2, dc2tog) 3 times (9)

Rnds 8-9 dc (2 rnds)

Rnd 10 (dc1, dc2tog) 3 times (6)

Rnds 11-12 dc (2 rnds)

Stuff lightly and sew flat into position.

HEAD PLUMAGE

Working in Black

Work three ch8 SLIP STITCH CHAINS (see page 19) onto top of head.

TAIL

Working in Ruby

Ch16 and sl st to join into a circle

Rnds 1-4 dc (4 rnds)

Change to Black

Rnds 5-6 dc (2 rnds)

Split into two rnds of 8 sts and work both as follows:

Rnds 1-4 dc (4 rnds)

Rnd 5 dc7, dc2 into next st (9)

Rnds 6-8 dc (3 rnds)

Rnd 9 dc8, dc2 into next st (10)

Rnds 10-12 dc (3 rnds)

Rnd 13 (dc4, dc2 into next st) twice (12) Rnds 14-16 dc (3 rnds)

Rnd 17 (dc2tog) 6 times (6)

Do not stuff.

Finish by sewing eyes into place with Black yarn.

THANKS

The birds for this book have been crocheted by a few sets of hands as we put our Christmas jumpers on, watched our favourite festive films and maybe ate a mince pie or two.

With huge thanks to the talented Evelyn Birch, for capturing my hands in these step-by-step illustrations, and for all her assistance making this book by sawing down Christmas trees and putting up fairy lights in February.

With special thanks to Jo Clements, Evelyn Birch and Rachel Critchley in enabling me to suddenly fly way beyond the four calling birds!

Further thanks are due to the rest of the TOFT team in supporting my creativity and delivering an exceptional experience to all of TOFT's customers around the world.

As ever, I could not continue to run a business and find time to develop books and have two young children without the understanding and support of my parents and Doug Lord.

A final thanks to my children for continuing to inspire me every day.

ABOUT THE AUTHOR

Kerry Lord is the founder of TOFT, a dynamic British yarn brand specialising in luxury wools and approachable patterns. Initially established with a focus on fashion-led knitting kits, Kerry first created the super popular Edward's Menagerie series of books in 2012, which have encouraged and taught thousands around the world to crochet for the first time.

TOFT continues to offer a strong design collection for both knitting and crochet: a commanding presence at craft shows all over the world, sell-out pattern subscription boxes (shipping internationally), and regular workshops at their Warwickshire HQ Studio make TOFT a big part of the contemporary craft scene, both in the UK and across the world.

Kerry enjoys collaborating and co-hosting ever-larger crochet events to bring new people to the craft, such as teaching 350 workshop attendees to make a whale at the Natural History Museum, London, and a touring exhibition of over 500 crochet animals bringing together the wider range in Edward's Menagerie.

TOFT is here to help if you are new to crochet and not sure where to begin, and the brand is based from a real place called Toft in Warwickshire, England. In addition to our yarns, TOFT now designs and manufactures a whole range of tools and accessories to accompany our crochet range.
www.toftuk.com @toft_uk #edsanimals

First published in the United Kingdom in 2020 by
Pavilion
An imprint of HarperCollinsPublishers
1 London Bridge Street
London SE1 9GF

www.harpercollins.co.uk

HarperCollinsPublishers
Macken House
39/40 Mayor Street Upper
Dublin 1
D01 C9W8
Ireland

Copyright © Pavilion 2020
Text and pattern/project copyright © Kerry Lord 2020

This book contains FSC™ certified paper and other controlled
sources to ensure responsible forest management. For more
information visit: www.harpercollins.co.uk/green

All rights reserved. No part of this publication may be copied,
displayed, extracted, reproduced, utilised, stored in a retrieval
system or transmitted in any form or by any means, electronic,
mechanical or otherwise including but not limited to photocopying,
recording, or scanning without the prior written permission of the
publishers.

The patterns contained in this book and the items created
from them are for personal use only. Commercial use of either the
patterns or items made from them is strictly prohibited.

ISBN 978-1-91166-326-3
A CIP catalogue record for this book is available
from the British Library.

10 9 8 7 6 5 4

Reproduction by Rival
Printed and bound by Papercraft, Malaysia

www.pavilionbooks.com

Publisher: Helen Lewis
Commissioning editor: Sophie Allen
Editor: Bella Cockrell
Design manager: Alice Kennedy-Owen
Photographer: Kristy Noble
Production manager: Phil Brown